Butterfly Swimming

THE VIKING LIBRARY OF SPORTS SKILLS

BUTTERFLY SWIMMING

DR. FRANK RYAN

THE VIKING PRESS / NEW YORK

Author's Note

Butterfly Swimming takes its place in the Viking Library of Sports Skills among three companion swimming books, *Freestyle Swimming*, *Breaststroke Swimming*, and *Backstroke Swimming*. All four books have common roots in that they are based on teaching films that are in use throughout most of the world. Two men have made essential contributions to both the films and the books. They are Phil Moriarty, Yale's famous varsity swimming coach, and Bob Reid, film expert and educator.

My personal enthusiasm for swimming has always existed, but it has grown with the preparation of these four films and four books. I join physical educators, physicians, and others concerned with health and recreation in the hope that one day everyone can enjoy swimming on a regular basis.

Although this book is concerned primarily with championship technique, it is hoped that it will benefit swimmers at every level of ability. It is always satisfying to improve performance, and the same techniques that make for world records make the rest of us go a little faster. After many years of coaching I am convinced that achievement is greatest when technique makes sense to the athlete. I trust this book reflects that point of view.

Preface

The butterfly stroke, the newest of the racing strokes, has a short history. Its emergence as a separate competitive stroke goes back only to 1952. It all began in Brooklyn in 1933. A swimmer named Henry Meyer experimented with an above-water recovery of the arms in the breaststroke. He reasoned that recovery of the arms through the air instead of through the water would eliminate practically all resistance to arm action. Not only would the arms recover more quickly, but the reduction of drag would allow the body to move faster. As the breaststroke rules were then written, the above-water recovery did not seem to be in violation. When the new stroke was first used in competition, it naturally brought great astonishment along with strong protest. However, Meyer's innovation was ruled to be legal. A new method was born, and nearly all breaststrokers adopted it. In the 1952 Olympic Games all of the finalists used butterfly arm action.

To preserve the breaststroke, the governing body for international swimming made the butterfly a separate stroke, and the dolphin kick was legalized. The frog kick still remains legal, but it is not used by the top competitors.

Even though the butterfly is an offshoot of the breaststroke, the arm action and the kick of the butterfly are very much like those of the crawl. At first sight the butterfly stroke doesn't seem to be much like the crawl because in the butterfly both the arms and the legs work simultaneously, but if we trace the pattern of one arm, we can see that the butterfly arm action and the crawl arm action are similar. The butterfly kick and the crawl kick are also fundamentally alike. However, because of the involvement of the body and the up-and-down movement of the hips, the kick of the butterfly is fuller and probably more powerful than that of the crawl kick. Because of the similarities between the two strokes, the freestyler usually takes to the butterfly very readily.

Since the butterfly developed from the breaststroke, the rules for the two events are similar. There is the same insistence on symmetry and simultaneous action. The arms must move together both in recovery and during the arm pull. They must also move symmetrically, which means that in addition to moving together they must be at about the same height. Briefly put, one arm should be pretty much the mirror image of the other. The same holds true for the legs. The rules permit "simultaneous movements of the legs and feet in the vertical plane." Both the frog kick and the dolphin kick are allowed, and it is permissible to switch from one kick to the other during a race.

As in the breaststroke, "the body must be kept perfectly on the breast, and both shoulders in the horizontal plane." This rule should not present any problem, since its violation would offer no advantage.

You have to hold form in touching both at the turn and in finishing the race. "When touching at the turn or in finishing a race, the touch shall be made with both hands simultaneously on the same level. The shoulders shall be in a horizontal position in line with the surface of the water."

There has been a remarkable improvement in butterfly performance. Today the top fliers can defeat very good freestylers. Butterfly records are beginning to approach those for the freestyle. Many coaches and swimmers feel that the butterfly is still an unexploited stroke and that great further progress can be expected. Some even think that the butterfly will eventually prove faster than the crawl stroke. This could be, but at the present time it doesn't seem likely. The crawl has a mechanical advantage over the butterfly in that the crawl's alternate actions of both the arms and the legs provide a fairly even application of power. In contrast, in the butterfly, because the arms and legs have to work simultaneously, there is a tendency toward powerful surges followed by dead spots. The experts are working to minimize the dead spots—a difficult job to carry out within the framework of the present rules.

All strokes require strength, but the butterfly is surely the most strenuous of the strokes. Great upper-body strength is needed to carry out the form correctly, so the flier puts greater emphasis on special land exercises.

Contents

Butterfly Swimming

Body Position

When anything moves, its speed depends on propulsion and resistance. There are forces that create movement and those that tend to retard movement. So it is with swimming, regardless of the stroke used. If there were no resistance, a single stroke would move you indefinitely and at the same speed. Resistance cannot be entirely eliminated, but it can be reduced by maintaining a streamlined body position that keeps water drag to a minimum.

The butterfly is a spectacular stroke, and it tends to create the illusion of extreme up-and-down movement of the body, which can mislead the beginner. Careful observation of the great butterflier, however, shows that there is relatively little up-and-down movement. The upper body stays at about the same level during the entire stroke, and the shoulders remain near the surface. Because of the dolphin kick, the hips do have a slight vertical movement. The downbeat drives the hips upward, and the upbeat's reaction lowers the hips. Yet the up-and-down movement of the hips doesn't cover much of a range—only a few inches.

Most resistance is created by nonalignment. In moving through the water a body can be out of alignment along any of three axes. It can fail to be level, it can be sideways—that is, not in line with the direction of move-ment—or it can rotate along its long axis. The last two possible interferences with streamlining should not bother the butterflier, because the symmetrical and simultaneous movements of the stroke should insure against both rolling and lateral nonalignment. Hence, the flier is free to concentrate

3

on keeping a level body position. The main task, then, is to keep the vertical movement of the body to a minimum. Any lowering of the body toward the vertical creates additional water resistance.

The biggest factor in stabilizing the body is the coordination between the action of the arms and the kick of the legs. Although the main function of the arms and legs is propulsive, their timing with each other is essential to efficient body position. Put briefly, the arms and legs can, with proper timing, counter each other's tendency to disturb body position. There will be a closer consideration of this timing in a later section.

The need to breathe always has some adverse effect on body position. At regular intervals the face has to be out of the water so that air can be taken in. In the butterfly stroke the interference with streamlining caused by breathing is minimized in two ways. First, the lifting of the head is timed with swimming action so that the breath is taken at a point when it least disturbs body position. Second, an effort is made to get the face out of the water without raising the upper body. This means that the neck muscles have to be used to lift the head.

Good body position can be described in fairly few words. This is particularly so in the case of the butterfly, because the streamlining problem exists with reference to only one aspect—keeping the body level. The description of good body position takes up only a small portion of this book, but that does not mean good body position is not important. Body position should always be emphasized. Keep in mind that even the most powerful arm pull and kick can be negated if the body position is not right.

1. The butterfly stroke is an undulating motion. The body plays an enormous part in propulsion, and at first glance it would seem that the flier is surging upward and downward. A careful look at these underwater photographs shows that up-and-down movement of the body does indeed exist but that it is not as extreme as it would appear—in fact, it can be measured in inches. The principle of keeping the best body position commensurate with effective propulsion is essential.

1a

1b

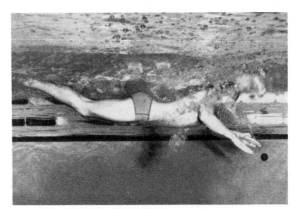

1c

1d

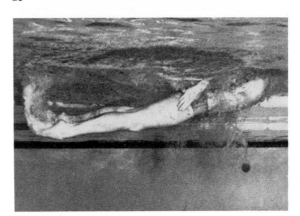

1e

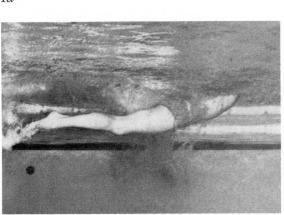

1f

Arm Action

At first glance, the arm action of the butterfly seems strange and puzzling, especially if the view is from an underwater window. However, it can be clearly understood on a logical basis. Actually, the arm action in the butterfly is like that of the crawl. It's just that when both arms work together they trace a curious pattern.

As with all strokes, the butterfly arm action can be best understood in terms of what we might call the paddle principle. Think of a canoe paddle. The paddle is driven backward through the water and in this way supplies forward propulsion. The force of propulsion depends on a number of factors, but for practical purposes speed and direction are what matters. Propulsion depends on action and reaction. This is true of everything that moves, including jet planes. Action and reaction are always in opposite directions, so we know that we want the action of the arms to cause a backward drive in order best to drive the body forward. This, then, is the base from which we start. We can then consider modifications in technique to take account of other factors, such as body position.

If we are going to use the paddle analogy as a way of understanding arm action, we have to take account of the structure of the paddle. What directly and finally matters is the broad blade of the paddle, the part that drives below the surface of the water and moves relatively fast.

For the most part it is the hand that functions as the blade, although during some portion of the stroke the forearm can move fast enough to contribute to propulsion. The contribution of the upper arms and the other

6

big muscles of the body is always indirect. Their job is to get the hands moving fast and in the right direction. Hence, strictly from the point of view of technique, our analysis of the arm stroke has to be concerned with what the hands are doing. Within such a framework let's take a look at the specifics of arm action.

The S pattern. Although there are slight variations, the general S pattern traced by hand is characteristic for all fine fliers. After the hands enter the water, the first movement is both outward and downward. The outward movement of the hands shifts smoothly to an inward movement. The hands come very close together at the point where they are directly under the shoulders. From then on, the hands move apart until the stroke is completed and the recovery begins.

The S pattern is a result of trying to make the arm stroke as efficient as possible throughout its entire length. The basic guiding principle is always action and reaction. We want the drive against the water to be as directly backward as possible. But we also have to take account of two other factors—body position and the ability to develop power. Perhaps a good way to understand the logic of the S pattern is to start with the idea that the arms could be kept straight and move directly backward in a vertical path during the full stroke. Then we can take a look at the modifications that are needed and the reasons for them.

When the hands enter the water, the arms are straight ahead in the direction in which the body is moving. Suppose the arms were kept straight and their first movement was directly downward. The downward action would produce an upward reaction, driving the body upward more than forward. There would be little contribution to forward speed, and there would be a loss of streamlining. Further, the arms would be in a poor mechanical position to exert power. The first part of such a stroke would therefore be clearly inefficient. However, efficiency would increase until the arms reached an up-and-down position. At this point the pull would be efficient—but only at this point. With the movement of the arms past the vertical position, the action would then become increasingly upward, forcing the body downward.

You can see that a straight-armed vertical pull cannot be truly efficient, because the action is directly backward at only one point. The goal of technique is to increase backward action over the entire arm stroke, and essential to reaching this goal is making use of the flexibility of the arms. By the appropriate bending of the arms the pull can be kept more backward, producing a greater forward reaction and thereby increasing the efficiency of the stroke.

Entry. As the arms finish their recovery, they are moving fast, and their speed should continue right into the water. Entry of the arms is almost straight ahead—they are just slightly to the outside. The palms are downward but turned enough so that the thumbs enter the water first. In this way the hands are in position to be blades for movement both outward and downward.

First part of the arm pull. As the outward-and-downward pull begins, the arms bend and the elbows are high. The bending of the arms and the raising of the elbows create a mechanical advantage, because the muscles quickly get into a favorable position to move the hands, which exert pressure against the water.

The hands come together. The hands reach their widest spread at about the time they are halfway to the downward vertical position. From there on, the hands start to come closer together, and the outward component gives way to an inward one. The elbows are kept high, while the hands rotate so that the palms face backward. As the hands come closer together, they can push more directly backward in alignment with the body. This is a highly efficient part of the stroke. At this point, because they are vertical, the forearms can also make a contribution to forward propulsion. The hands are closest together when the arms are directly beneath the body.

Past the vertical. After coming close together, the hands continue to sweep backward and outward. As the forearms lose their vertical position, they make less of a contribution to forward propulsion. The hands, however, continue to push the water directly backward. Flexion of the wrists permits the hands to be straight up and down almost to the very end of the stroke. The palms continue to act as efficient paddleblades. The outward, or rounded, action of the arms toward the finish of the stroke helps prepare for the recovery. If the arms were going straight back, they would have to stop to begin forward movement, but the rounded action allows the hands as they leave the water to maintain continuity of movement. The arms keep right on going.

Recovery. The final action of the arms in the water is really an anticipation of the recovery. Even before the hands leave the water, the arms are already starting to recover. No time is lost in making the recovery. The rounded action of the arms adds to momentum and ensures that the finish of the stroke blends smoothly into the recovery so that there is continuity of action.

The recovery is made above but close to the water. The hands literally skim over the water. Extra height of the hands would be wasteful of energy, and it would interfere with efficient form. Since there is no water resistance during the recovery, the arms can move fast and, at the same time, be re-laxed. Power for the recovery comes from the muscles of the shoulders and upper back, and once the initial thrust has been made by these muscles, the arms can coast forward. When the hands leave the water, the palms are toward the rear. They rotate easily and smoothly during the recovery so that the fingers are pointing almost directly forward at entry. As the hands enter the water, it is important that the arms retain their momentum. Continuity of movement is essential both to body position and the efficiency of the stroke.

Breathing. The movement required for breathing is bound to interfere with streamlining. The goal is to keep this interference to a minimum while, of course, still taking in an adequate amount of air. To inhale air the face has to be lifted partially out of the water. The best technique is to lift the head without lifting the entire upper body. The neck is stretched backward so that most of the face is above the water. At this point, the eyes are looking straight ahead and the head is brought no higher than necessary, the chin remaining in the water. The beginner may have to lift his head a little higher to avoid taking in water, but with experience he will learn to keep his head fairly low and still avoid the intake of water.

The best time to lift the head is when the shoulders are highest, and even with an efficient arm stroke its early action causes some lifting of the upper body. The upward reaction of the arm action is completed at about the time that the arms reach the vertical. This is the most favorable point for the head to rise so that a breath can be taken. Inhalation is fast so that the head can quickly return to swimming position, and the breath is held to increase buoyancy. Exhalation occurs just before the next inhalation. Frequency of breathing, as in the crawl stroke, is usually determined by the length of the race. In most races breathing is carried out every two or three strokes. But some swimmers breathe every stroke. Apparently the breathing pattern is an individual matter, each swimmer finding the pattern that suits him best.

2. The powerful butterfly arm pull traces an *S* pattern.

2a

2d

2e

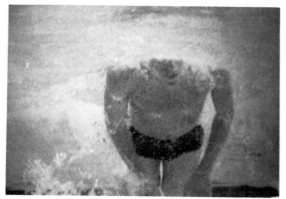

2h

3. Because the butterfly stroke is continuous and rhythmic, the arm pull blends into the recovery. The arms finish their drive and skim forward close to the surface of the water. With no water resistance during the recovery, the arms have a good chance to relax. The powerful muscles of the trunk supply the impetus (d). After the intake of air has been completed, the head is again in the water to aid streamlining.

3a

2b

2c

2f

2g

3b

3c

3d

3e

4. Breathing is co-ordinated with the arm action. To preserve good body position the neck muscles are used to raise the face out of the water. The intake of air is carried out quickly and the face is again lowered.

4a

4b

The Dolphin Kick

The legs are a powerful part of the body. They are at least twice as strong as the arms, and they have much greater endurance. You can move around all day on your legs—and for only a matter of seconds on your arms. Runners depend entirely on their legs for propulsion; the arms have only a balancing effect. In swimming, however, the arms are the main source of propulsion, and the legs are used primarily for balance.

Because the legs represent such an enormous potential source of power, swimming experts have always been frustrated by their inability to make better use of them. The dolphin kick—which, as indicated by its name, is meant to simulate the powerful swimming action of the dolphin—may represent a partial solution.

The mechanics of running are not entirely simple, but compared to swimming they are relatively easy to grasp. In running only the feet are in contact with the medium. All effort is intended to build up the speed of the feet against the ground. A much more complicated situation exists in swimming, and although we don't have to be too concerned with the complications, it is helpful to note a few of them. The most obvious one is that both the hands and the feet are propelling surfaces. Another is that the forearms and forelegs, during parts of their action, also become propelling surfaces. Of course, there is an enormous complication in that, unlike the runner, who moves on the surface, the swimmer is moving *through* the water. That means that the swimmer has to pay as much attention to the water resistance he creates as he does to the propulsive power he develops. Kicking, then, is not the simple act it may at first appear to be. It is realistic and helpful to mention the complications that exist, because their analysis will contribute to more effective technique, but for our purposes now it is enough to remember that the arms are the primary source of propulsion.

In swimming there are two main sources of propulsion for moving the same body—the arms and the legs. Each can work alone to move the body forward, but combining their actions may or may not increase forward speed. It is clear enough that the arms are the primary source of speed, so we must see in what ways the kick can increase the speed that arm action alone can build up. To put it briefly, the legs must operate in such a way that they get the feet moving backward faster than the body is moving forward. That may sound a little complicated, but let's take a further look. If the arms alone can generate a forward body speed of four miles per hour, the kick can make a contribution to propulsion only when the feet are moving backward faster than four miles per hour. Of course, the faster the better. Anything less than four miles per hour would create drag, or water resistance.

In addition to foot speed there are other factors in assessing the efficiency of the kick. The kick has to be made in such a way as to keep water resistance low. The legs could produce propulsive foot speed and, at the same time, nullify the gain by also producing excessive drag. The kick has still another important function. It helps to stabilize body position and thus contributes to streamlining.

A look at the dolphin kick. The dolphin kick is very likely the most powerful of all the swimming kicks. The entire body seems to contribute to the power of the drive, as the body and legs perform like a whip in building up great velocity of the feet. Unlike other strokes where hip position is fixed, the hips move up and down in the dolphin kick. This hip mobility is a significant feature in developing power.

Because the arms pull together rather than alternately, there is no roll of the body. The kicking action is straight up and down. There is no diagonal component as in the kicking action for the crawl or backstroke because there is no need to compensate for or adjust to a body roll.

Just as the arm action of the butterfly is similar to that of the crawl stroke, the kicks of the two strokes have the same basic features. Of course, there is the obvious difference that in the dolphin kick both legs move together, not alternately. The dolphin kick is fuller and more powerful, the increased range of the kick coming about through hip mobility.

When carried out well, the dolphin kick is smooth, undulating, and continuous. It does indeed resemble the graceful swimming of the dolphin. Even though the dolphin kick should be a continuous action, it is useful for the purposes of analysis to break it down into two parts—the upbeat and the downbeat.

Upbeat. The upbeat has to be viewed primarily as a preparation for the powerful downbeat. Most experienced coaches believe that the upbeat can make no direct contribution to forward propulsion, but that it has two alternate functions. First, it prepares for the downbeat. Second, the reaction of the upbeat helps to stabilize body position. The argument is that since the upbeat can make no contribution to body speed, the main concentration should be on raising the legs with a minimum of water resistance. In brief, the upbeat cannot help propel the body forward, but it should not hinder by creating unnecessary drag.

Actually, there is some evidence that the upbeat can make a contribution to forward speed. Definitive studies are difficult to come by, and the matter may remain in doubt for some time to come. However, the test of contribution to propulsion is basically simple. As we have stated, if you can get the feet moving backward faster than the body is moving forward, there is a contribution to speed. Slow-motion movies of some fine swimmers suggest that this can be done. Among the top performers, especially those with good ankle flexibility, water pressure during the upbeat bends the ankle so that the sole of the foot is facing backward, which could not happen unless the legs were contributing to forward speed. Without such a contribution the ankles would flex in the opposite direction so that the toes would point backward. In any case, the upbeat should be carried out with the intention of making a contribution to forward speed.

At the end of the downbeat the hips are high and the legs are straight. This position comes about naturally as a result of the downbeat. The legs are kept straight as they start upward. It's important that there be no bend at the knees, because a bend would cause drag. Some loose-jointed swimmers can even gain from hyperextension, a "reverse bend" at the knees. The ankles flex so that the soles of the feet are facing backward. This position of the feet allows the important backward push against the water. The upbeat ends when the legs are about parallel to the surface of the water.

Downbeat. The downward movement of the legs is the obvious source of power. In whipping downward the legs build up to a fast and powerful backward thrust of the feet. The speed of the downbeat can be so great that even the forelegs contribute to propulsion. The power of the downbeat is due to the construction of the legs. The legs can straighten with great power; the extensor muscles of the thighs are capable of enormous drive.

At the finish of the upbeat, the legs are still straight. Because of the reaction created by the upward movement of the legs, the hips are at their highest point. The downbeat is begun by a downward movement of the upper legs. The lower legs continue their upward movement, rising almost to the surface. This combination of actions causes the knees to bend, and at the point of fullest bend the upper leg and foreleg form approximately a right angle. After maximum leg bend has been reached, the forelegs start downward. At the same time, the upper legs continue their downward drive. The whip is ready to be cracked. The lower legs, already moving fast, now receive terrific momentum from the straightening of the legs.

Ankle flexibility is vital. Although the forelegs can and should contribute to forward propulsion, the feet are the main blades. It's not enough for the feet to be moving fast; they must be positioned to push the water backward. A different part of the foot is used for the downbeat. Remember that during the upbeat it is the soles of the feet that are driven backward. During the downbeat it is the insteps, or tops of the feet, that are the pushing surfaces. This calls for an extreme change of foot position. Looseness or flexibility of the ankles is the key, because if the ankles are loose enough, water pressure positions the feet correctly.

The more direct is the backward drive, the greater is the contribution to forward propulsion. But there is always a downward action, and the reaction raises the hips to the surface. The legs are fully extended at the end of the downbeat, and you are ready to begin the upbeat. The action is continuous and flowing, with the downbeat blending into the upbeat and, in turn, the upbeat blending into the downbeat.

5. As a result of the dolphin kick, the hips move up and down. This movement is a natural reaction to the kicking motion and also makes the kick more powerful. The up-and-down movement is not as extreme as it appears. Check the pool line in the background for an idea of the range of hip movement.

5a

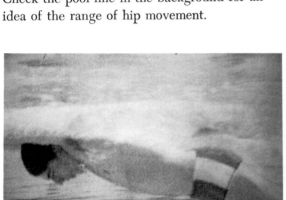

5b

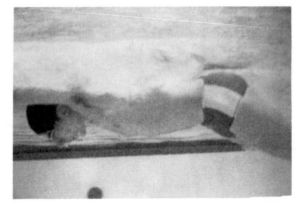

5c

5d

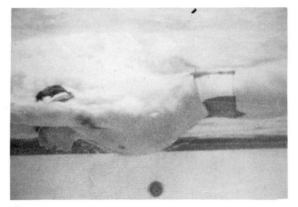

5e

6. It's velocity and positioning of the feet that count. The feet must not only be moving fast; they must be pointed in the right direction so that the push is backward. The feet will tend to push the water backward if the ankles are loose.

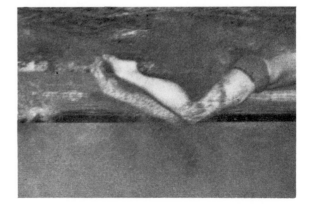

7. The downbeat of the dolphin kick is a powerful smash that should build up great velocity of the feet. Although the upbeat may make some contribution to propulsion, it is primarily a preparation for the downbeat. The goal is to develop a whiplike action of the body and legs that results in the feet moving fast.

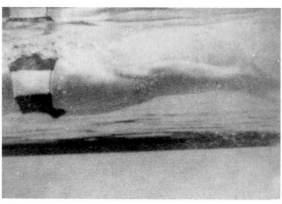

7a

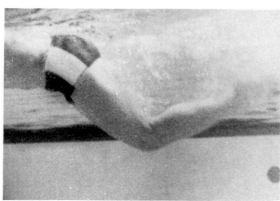

7d

7e

7h

8. The dolphin kick—here somewhat exaggerated by use of the kickboard—represents a powerful build-up of energy which propels the body forward. In (b) the propelling power of the feet is clearly seen.

8a

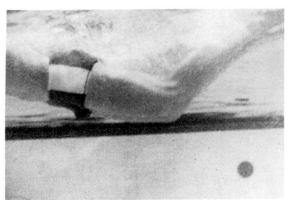

7b

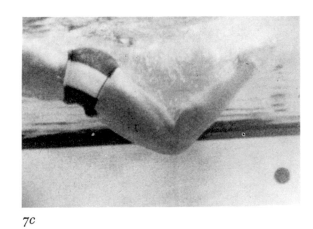

7c

7f

7g

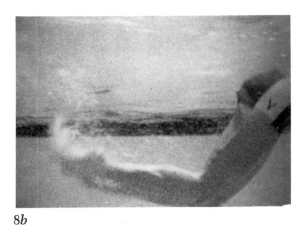

8b

8c

Co-ordinating the Arms and Legs

In timing arm action with the kick there are two primary goals: reducing "dead spots" in propulsion and maintaining good body position. In the four competitive strokes the ratio of arm pulls to leg kicks varies over a considerable range. For the breaststroke the ratio is one to one. That is, for each arm pull there is one kick. For the crawl and backstroke the ratio is one to six, or one arm pull to six beats of the legs. In the butterfly there is one simultaneous pull of the arms for every two kicks. There is nothing magical or forever fixed about the ratio of any of the four strokes. Experimentation continues as coaches and swimmers look for more effective techniques, and we may see some changes, especially in the crawl and backstroke. However, in the case of the butterfly the ratio of one arm pull to two kicks seems likely to remain unchanged. There are compelling reasons for this ratio.

Let's look at the timing between the arms and the legs in the butterfly and the reasons for it. A useful starting place is at the point of full recovery as the arms are just entering the water. Because the arms have been recovering rather than driving, there is a tendency for the body to lose speed—to hit a "dead spot." This relative slowing down presents a good opportunity for the kick to be effective. Remember that the effectiveness of the kick depends on driving the feet backward faster than the body is moving forward, so the kick is most effective at the body's slowest speed. The downbeat of the legs begins just as the arm pull begins.

In addition to taking advantage of the relative slowdown of the body, the kick helps to stabilize the body. Even with ideal form the pull of the arms cannot be entirely backward. There is always some forward component to the pull. The downward action of the pull produces an upward reaction which tends to lift the upper body. A lifting of the upper body would drop the lower body, and the resulting position would increase water resistance. But the downward thrust of the legs lifts the hips, counteracting the tendency for the hips to drop. The total result is that the body tends to remain level, and a streamlined position is maintained.

The second downbeat of the legs takes place during the last portion of the arm stroke. At this point, the body is moving at its fastest, and the kick has less chance to contribute to forward propulsion. You will recall the basic principle that in order to contribute to forward speed the pushing area must move backward faster than the body is moving forward. Obviously, the faster the body is moving the more difficult it is to meet this requirement. Hence, the second kick cannot contribute as much to forward propulsion as the first kick does.

The important function of the second downbeat of the legs is to help maintain body stability, to counteract the effects produced by the last part of the arm action. As the hands and forearms reach the vertical, the arm stroke is at its most efficient because the water is being pushed almost directly backward, but past the vertical point both the hands and the forearms are moving upward as well as backward. This upward action produces a downward reaction, which tends to lower the hips. Were it not for the neutralizing effect of the kick, the hips would drop, and there would be increased drag or water resistance. At this critical point the downbeat causes an upward reaction. With proper timing the reactions produced by the arms and legs cancel each other, and the body tends to remain in a streamlined position.

In summary, then, the two-beat kick of the butterfly serves two important purposes—propulsion and streamlining of the body. In attaining these goals timing is important. The first kick comes when it can contribute maximum propulsion and also help maintain good body position. The second kick contributes less to movement, because the downbeat is made when the body is moving at its greatest speed, but it is important to preserve streamlining.

9. In this sequence the double function of the dolphin kick is seen. As the arms are recovering and the body is slowing down (c, d, and e), the kick has its best chance to be effective. Another kick compensates for the lifting of the body by the arms (f, g, and h).

9*a*

9*d*

9*e*

9*h*

10. This sequence demonstrates the ability of the dolphin kick to stabilize the body as well as provide power. The second kick per arm cycle, shown here, is the one that counteracts the downward reaction of the arm pull and so helps to keep the body level.

10*c*

10*d*

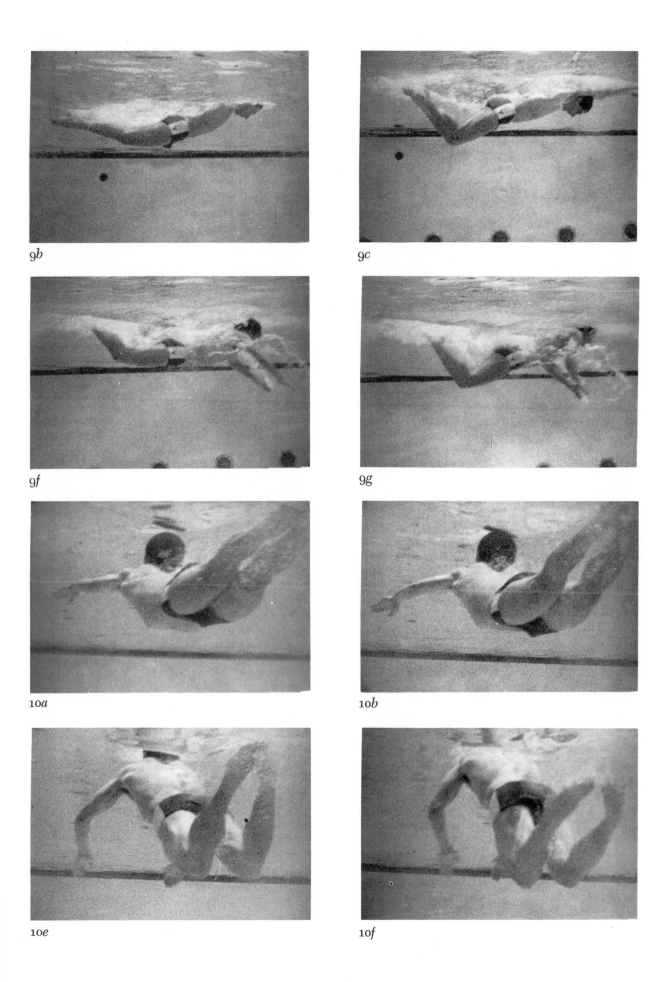

9b

9c

9f

9g

10a

10b

10e

10f

10g

10h

10i

10j

11. As the arms are partly through the powerful pull, the legs, seen here from the rear, are positioning for the strong blow that will both maintain body position and contribute to forward propulsion.

11a

11b

11c

The Start

The butterfly start is the same as that used in the crawl stroke, and, except for the angle of entry into the water, it is also similar to that of the breast-stroke. Before turning to the butterfly, most swimmers begin with either the crawl stroke or the breaststroke, or both. Hence, all the practice effort in starting for these two strokes has carry-over value for the butterfly start.

You may already be familiar with the techniques of starting, which are not difficult to understand. What matters most are the practice time and effort given to them. Most fine swimmers are now thoroughly convinced that the start is a vital part of a race and are willing to give the start the practice attention it deserves.

Unfortunately, even now some experts take the position that somehow the start will automatically work itself out, that a reasonably good start will come about without direct attention. It may be true that a fairly good start can be worked out without intensive attention to detail, but a fairly good start isn't enough in an era when place winners are so close at the finish line that they often have to be separated by electronic devices.

Making the most of a solid surface. Man can move about five times faster on land than he can through the water. That's because he can create a greater reaction driving against a solid surface than he can by driving against liquid. The swimmer has the opportunity to use a solid surface only at the start and during the turns, and both opportunities should be thoroughly exploited. Our present concern is with the start.

The goals of the start. Realistic measures of a start's effectiveness are speed and distance. You want to get out fast and far. In practice starts against teammates and in actual competition you will get a good idea of where you stand. If you're behind when you surface, you know that a lot has to be done. If you are even, that's not good enough. If you are ahead, it's encouraging that you have an edge—but the job is to work to make the edge even greater. Another way to evaluate your performance is to have your speed checked by a stopwatch.

The start should be a smooth co-ordinated act. One part blends into and influences the next part. Basically, there are four goals of the start. First, it's important to react quickly to the gun. Second, you want to develop power off the blocks for speed and distance. Third, you want to enter the water in as knifelike a manner as possible so that there is minimum resistance. Fourth, once in the water, you should maintain a streamlined position of the body to take advantage of the speed you have generated.

"Take your mark." At the starter's command you move easily into place. The rules require only that you hold a steady position. Feet are spaced comfortably, between six and twelve inches apart. The toes grip the edge of the starting platform to afford a firmer base for the drive. There is a slight bend to the knees, and body weight is balanced over the balls of the feet. The body is bent forward, and the arms hang loosely. It is important to be relaxed, yet at the same time to concentrate on movement. A great body of experimental literature demonstrates that reaction time is faster when attention is on the move to be made rather than on the stimulus.

When the gun sounds. With enough practice and with concentration on movement, the sound of the gun puts you into action. The body moves forward, and at the same time the arms, kept fairly straight, begin their circular swing. In this way the arms develop greater momentum and are co-ordinated better with the body's downward and forward movement. During the first part of their swing, the arms are wide, but as they descend, they move close to the body. They continue their vigorous swing until just before they become parallel to the surface of the water. At this point arm movement is stopped, and the momentum of the arms is transferred to the body.

The legs increase their bend, the increased flexion at the knees serving two important purposes. The bend helps to lower the body, and it allows the legs to be better prepared for a powerful drive off the platform. The knees reach their maximum bend at about the time that the arms are swinging past the legs on their way forward. From this point on, the legs begin to straighten while keeping contact with the platform. The legs continue their drive, and the body continues to lower as it straightens. When the leg drive is completed and contact with the platform is broken, the body is extended and almost parallel to the water's surface. The arms are forward.

Entry. An efficient entry preserves the speed that has been generated off the starting platform. This means creating the least possible resistance upon entering the water. The body literally forms a straight line from outstretched hands to outstretched toes, with the head between the arms. The hands enter the water first. Body position is held. This is one of the rare times when relaxation is not useful. The body must be held rather stiffly so that its streamlining is not disturbed.

The angle of entry is now obviously important, but not so long ago, when it was thought that the body should land completely flat or parallel to the water, swimmers used the so-called racing start. There was a great splash, with the arms "contributing" by vigorously slapping the water. The unfortunate idea was to avoid sinking in the water, there being a peculiar illusion that the swimmer could remain on the surface after the start. Further, it was believed that he could and should start swimming immediately. Observation and experience have made it absolutely clear that a completely flat dive causes loss of body speed and is otherwise harmful. All coaches now recognize that the start should bring you underwater. It is possible, however, to dive too deeply, and in such a case valuable time is lost in getting back to the surface. It takes practice and experience to get a feel for the right angle of entry.

In the water. No matter what the stroke, the start, because it is made against a solid surface, always develops speed that is greater than swimming speed. The logic of making the best use of a glide that is faster than swimming speed is compelling. It's easy to see that a premature effort to swim not only slows you down but also takes away the valuable relaxation that the glide should provide. This principle is easy enough to grasp but is usually difficult to put into practice. Patience and poise are the critical factors. Particularly among beginners, there is a strong tendency under the excitement of competition to try to start swimming immediately, but training and experience produce the poise that lets you follow the basic principle: swimming starts only when the speed of the glide slows down to swimming speed.

It is possible to start swimming too late, but this is an unusual error, and when it does occur, it results from too steep an entry, so that glide speed becomes less than swimming speed before the surface is reached. Too much depth can be partially corrected by positioning the arms and head to guide the body upward.

Future starting techniques. Except for the backstroke, starting rules are not very restricting, the basic requirement being that the swimmer "hold a steady balance for an appreciable length of time." That gives the swimmer a lot of leeway in taking a starting position, so changes in starting technique may be seen in the future.

Considerable attention is being given to the "grab" start, which a number of swimmers are using in top-level competition. It follows the lead offered by sprinters in track a few generations ago. In the grab start the arms, instead of simply hanging downward, are lowered so that the hands can grasp the underside of the starting platform. The head is low, so that the line of vision is almost directly downward.

This start is intended to increase the amount of crouch, lowering the body's center of gravity and thus shortening the interval between the sound of the gun and the final leg drive. The leg drive can be efficient only when the body is low enough for the major thrust to be forward rather than upward. The idea is that the grab start immediately places the body in the lowered position. There is no waiting for gravity to do the job. Surely the idea has merit. However, the grab start does not lower the body's center of gravity all that much. At the present time the future of the grab start is still in doubt, but this new method is worth watching.

Improvements in starting technique may not arrive in a dramatic or radical way. There may be a series of gradual refinements, each making the start slightly more efficient. However, they can add up to a significant result.

12. The start of the butterfly is the same as that used in freestyle swimming. The basic goals are to get away fast, develop power, and enter the water in a streamlined position.

12a

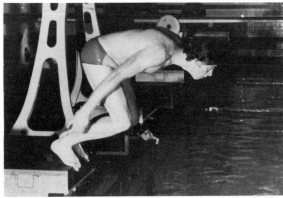

12b

12c

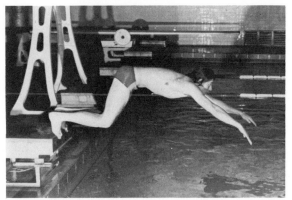

12d

12e

12f

13. While the body is falling toward efficient driving position, the circular and vigorous action of the arms develops power. The arms continue to swing until they are in line with the body. They then stop, and their energy is transferred to the body to increase forward movement.

13a

13d

13e

14. Great interest is now being shown in the grab start. It is thought that an advantage can be gained by having the body's center of gravity lower when the gun sounds. A disadvantage may be the lessened arm action, and more experience with this start is needed. All ambitious swimmers, however, will want to follow the findings concerning the effectiveness of this new technique.

14a

13b

13c

13f

14b

14c

The Turn

A turn represents a great opportunity for increased speed. Of course, this opportunity is open to all competitors, so it's best to assume that your opponents are also going to try to make the most of the opportunity the turn presents. That means your turn has to be efficient so that you don't give away any advantage. Better yet, make it your goal to polish your turn so that you gain an advantage.

The tests of a good turn are two. First, is the turn made within the rules? Second, is the turn as fast as possible?

Rules. What the rules really amount to is that you must be swimming butterfly form when you touch the wall and return to butterfly form before you lose contact with the wall. Specifically, the rules state:

> When touching at the turn or in finishing a race, the touch shall be made with both hands simultaneously on the same level, and with the shoulders in the horizontal plane. Once a legal touch has been made, the contestant may turn in any manner desired, but the prescribed form must be attained before the feet leave the wall in the push-off.
>
> When a contestant is in the underwater position after the start, when turning, or during the race, he is allowed to make one or more kicks.

Disqualification, of course, means loss of the race. Even if you have a large lead and are doing everything else well, all is in vain if you are disqualified.

The feeling is even worse if you disqualify your relay team. Hence the need to be aware of the rules at all times when you are practicing the turn. A good policy is to try never to make a practice turn that violates the rules, so there will be no probability of disqualification. In this way you will be freer to concentrate on technique and speed.

Speed. Obviously you want the turn to be as fast as possible, but the significant speed is not simply that of the body's changing direction. Both the speed of the approach and the speed off the wall are essential. To get a realistic measure of the speed of your turn, we would have to select a spot perhaps some ten yards or so from the wall and then time you from the time you pass this spot on your way to the wall until you pass it again on your return from the wall. The time would reflect the efficiencies of the major components of the turn: the approach, the pivot at the wall, and the drive off the wall.

Nearing the wall. An efficient approach to the wall calls for good timing. Ideally, the arms should be extended and ready to make the touch. This means that you should be at the wall just as the arms are completing the recovery, at which point they are extended forward. The obvious errors in timing are nearing the wall during the arm pull or getting there too long after the arms have recovered. In the first case, by the time the arms can recover and extend you can literally be jammed against the wall and unable to operate efficiently. In the other case, you have already recovered, and you have to wait for the body's momentum to bring your hands to the wall. When this happens, there is an obvious loss of speed.

The solution to the problem of timing lies in practice. Through countless practice turns you can develop a "feel" that brings you to the wall at the right time. You learn almost unconsciously and instinctively to make slight adjustments during the last several strokes. The lifting of the head during air intake lets you perceive the distance to the wall.

At the wall. The rules are of prime importance. Both hands must touch the wall together and at the same level. The shoulders must be horizontal when the touch is made. After you satisfy the rules, you can turn any way you want to. You just have to back in a correct position before you leave the wall. The rules for the turn are similar to those for the breaststroke, and so is the technique of turning.

Upon making contact with the wall there are two basic jobs for the arms to do—push and lift. The pushing task is the more important of the two. The lifting movement is made easier if there is a gutter to be grasped. Lacking a gutter, the deck of the pool can be used if it is low enough. In some pools there may be only the wall to work with.

When the hands reach the wall, the bend of the arms is partial. They have a slight "give." One arm does the work against the wall, while the other contributes to the turn by whipping around toward the opposite end of the pool. Which hand works against the wall and which hand whips is, of course, determined by whether you want to turn to the right or to the left. The direction selected is a matter of personal preference, but for ease of description let's assume you are turning to the right. Upon contact the arms push down to lift the upper body. The lifting movement of the right arm is very brief, because the right arm quickly leaves the wall to begin its whipping action.

When the touch is made, the legs begin to tuck under to make the body more compact. The turning radius is reduced, and the body is able to turn faster and more easily. The legs maintain their flexed position until the feet are placed solidly against the wall.

While the legs are doing their jobs of tucking and positioning themselves against the wall, the arms continue to work, with one arm pushing and the other whipping about. Once the arms have completed their contribution to the turning movements, their goal is to attain position for effective stream-lining of the body. The arms move forward so that the head is between them. In the final position the arms are straight and parallel to the surface of the water with the hands close together.

During the turn the lifting action of the arms brings the head out of the water—but just out of the water, not much more. An effective rule is to lift the body just enough so that a breath can be taken in. It's easy to see that extra lifting wastes energy and also interferes with carrying out correct technique.

The tests for a good turn, then, are legality and efficiency. The two points of possible disqualification are at the touch and upon leaving the wall. Using the turning technique described in this section, you should have no problem in staying within the rules. It will come to your attention that some outstanding swimmers have been experimenting with a riskier type of turning method. The fastest kind of turn is, of course, the somersault turn used in freestyle swimming, because for all practical purposes there are no restrictions on the freestyle turn. There doesn't even have to be a hand touch. It's natural enough for fliers to eye the freestyle turn with the hope that they can make use of its features and still not risk disqualification. It doesn't seem useful, at this point, to get involved in a full description of the flip or somersault turn, but we can mention the major difficulty in carrying out such a turn while staying within the rules for the butterfly stroke. In making the somersault turn, because there is really only a half somersault, there has to be a rotation of the body. It's very hard to squeeze in this rotation between the two points of wall touch and departure from the wall. There is a natural tendency to start the rotation before the touch—which calls for disqualification. And there is a similar natural tendency to complete the rotation of the body after breaking contact with the wall—which also calls for disqualification. In summary, the turn used by the great majority of fliers presents very little problem of disqualification. The experimental turns are risky, but they should be watched.

The other and obvious test of the turn is its speed. But, as mentioned earlier, any measure of speed should reflect the overall picture, including the speed of approach to the wall. That's why the speed of the turn should be timed from a selected point considerably away from the wall, ten yards or so.

All aspects of the turn deserve attention. However, a significant checkpoint occurs as the body is ready to drive off the wall. The body should, of course, be fully turned and in the new direction of swimming. The legs should be flexed, with the feet in solid contact with the wall. The arms are forward to aid in streamlining. Reaching an effective push-off suggests that the turn is being carried out at least reasonably well.

Off the wall. The leg drive off the wall should be as full and as powerful as possible. The use of a solid surface to push against presents the opportunity to generate great speed, and for this reason an attempt to swim immediately would produce water resistance. It's important to remember that initial glide speed should be greater than swimming speed. Hence, after the push off the wall, the first job is to hold a streamlined position. Swimming starts only when the glide speed slows to swimming speed. Some swimmers prefer to start with the kick alone, while others begin with leg and arm action together.

Similarity to the breaststroke turn. The butterfly rules are the same as those for the breaststroke, and the techniques for the two turns are similar. The main differences are timing and depth in the water. The timing of the butterfly turn is faster, because you are approaching the wall at greater speed, and the legs are in a better position for a quicker tuck. The butterfly turn is shallower than the breaststroke turn. In leaving the wall the breaststroke swimmer needs greater depth to take advantage of the rules. The butterfly swimmer doesn't require this depth.

15. These are the basic features of the turn: The wall is approached at full speed (a). Timing is important and comes from practice. The hands touch the wall together and at the same level according to the rules (b). The body tucks to make the turn faster and easier (c). Leg drive determines the speed off the wall (d and e). The streamlined position is resumed (f), and the speed generated by the drive of the legs is held patiently until the body slows to swimming speed (g).

15a

15d

15e

15*b*

15*c*

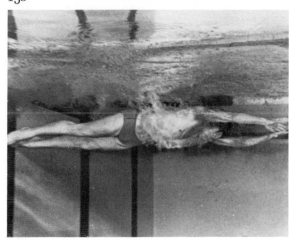

15*f*

15*g*

16. A full action sequence of the turn shows the essentials in detail. The first requirement is that the touch satisfy the rules (a). The wall is approached at full speed, and the turning action starts immediately (b). A fast turn depends on both the arm action and the tucking of the body (c, d, and e). The legs reach a power position against the wall (f), and the drive of the legs generates great speed (g, h, and i). Back to correct position (j), streamlining is held to maintain speed (k, l, and m) until the start of swimming (n).

16a

16d

16e

16h

16i

16l

16m

16*b*

16*c*

16*f*

16*g*

16*j*

16*k*

16*n*

17a

17. The pushing hand completes a powerful drive off the wall and then whips around to a forward position.

17d

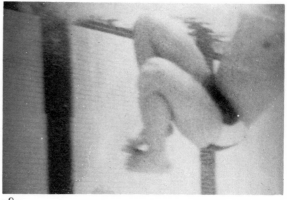

18a

18. Leg placement is critical in an effective turn. The feet are placed solidly against the wall with the legs bent.

18d

17b

17c

18b

18c

Training

The "lonely distance runner" does exist, but seldom is there a "lonely swimmer." The distance runner can train almost anywhere—in the field, woods, hills, or on the dunes of a beach. But a swimmer needs a pool, and exclusive use of a pool is a rarity. There are bound to be other swimmers practicing with you, but that's to the good, because you will profit from their presence in many ways. Of even more value is a good coach, and it is hoped you will have the luck to find one who is imaginative and competent.

A coach can bring his knowledge and experience to bear in planning effective workout for you, and the modern coach will also want you to understand the thinking behind the workout he prescribes. He knows that if you understand the principles and methods on which he draws there will be an increase in your satisfaction, enthusiasm, and progress. He has found that all great swimmers have a good grasp of training principles and that this understanding has contributed to their achievement.

Because of scientific findings and other observations, our knowledge of the conditioning process has greatly expanded during the last generation. The search for even more improved methods goes on, of course, but our present methods provide a highly valuable base for setting up effective workouts.

Work. Our most useful scientific discoveries are those that tell us how work is best carried out. The realization that we can profit from a lot of work is in itself highly significant. We are not nearly so delicate as the experts once thought, and the athletes of today work many times harder

42

than the athletes of the past. Even our young girl swimmers swim several times the mileage of yesteryear's male champions—and their performances are better.

Sheer work alone, however, does not ensure a good job of conditioning. Work has to be applied in the right doses. The body adjusts to a remarkable workload in conditioning, but it must be given a chance. The increase in work must be gradual or progressive. Because the strenuous workout schedules of the great swimmers often receive publicity, there is a natural tendency for the beginner to try to copy these rugged schedules immediately; however, the result of this imitative effort can be both discouraging and harmful. It's important to remember that the demanding workouts of the champions result from a gradual build-up.

About conditioning. Over the years the word "conditioning" has come to have various meanings for different people. In the strictest sense conditioning should have reference to a specific task. The purist might ask, "Conditioning for what?" Conditioning should perhaps refer to all of the factors, physical and psychological, that affect the ability to perform in a particular activity. For the swimmer, conditioning can include many types of adjustment. For example, part of the mental adjustment is increased tolerance of pain and fatigue. However, in this section we will be primarily concerned with the physiological aspects of conditioning—that is, developing the strength and endurance needed for good performance.

From the standpoint of physical conditioning, swimming may well be the best of all sports activities. Swimming both requires and generates a nice balance of strength and endurance. Nearly all the muscles of the body are used, and regular swimming makes them stronger and more capable of sustained effort. Even more important, the heart and lungs become increasingly efficient.

As you would expect, constant repetition of a task will make you better at that task. For example, if the task is to swim one hundred yards at your best speed, you could concentrate on swimming one-hundred-yard races during every training period. Such a program would bring about a certain amount of improvement. But the curious and highly significant finding is that you can become much better through the use of training methods that might seem indirect. We will be reviewing these methods and suggesting the ways in which they are incorporated into day-to-day workouts.

In analyzing an athletic event it isn't always easy to separate strength from endurance, since both qualities are required for athletic performance. The event itself determines the relative emphasis to be placed on either quality. All swimming events require endurance, but it is clear enough that the ratio of strength to endurance would be greater for the 50-yard sprint than for the 1500-meter race. In short, all swimmers train for both strength and endurance, but sprinters put more emphasis on strength, while distance swimmers place greater emphasis on endurance.

Strength. Swimming is never strictly a power event, such as the shot-put in track and field, in which performance depends on an enormous burst of power over a very short period of time. In swimming, even a sprinter, who needs great strength, must have endurance to sustain his speed. The fine sprinters tend to be strong athletes who increase their natural strength through special exercise programs.

Assuming body position to be constant, a swimmer's speed through the water depends almost entirely on how fast he can move his arms and feet in a backward direction. As the arms pull, they meet the resistance of the water. The greater the speed of the arms, the greater is the water resistance to be overcome. The stronger the swimmer's arms, the more they can overcome resistance and the faster they can be pulled through the water.

Strength-building depends on a program of progressive resistance. Gradually and regularly the resistance presented to the muscles is increased. After a certain point is reached, swimming does not lend itself too well to strength-building, the difficulty being that it is not feasible to bring about regular and significant increases in resistance. When the full stroke is used, the only way to increase resistance is to swim faster. Hence, the increments are not likely to be either reliable or significant. However, the arms and legs can be isolated in turn and the "overload" principle used. If the legs are tied, the burden of propulsion falls completely on the arms. In this way resistance is increased above that of normal swimming. The situation is reversed by using a kickboard and making the legs do all of the work.

Strength is best developed by land exercises. A countless number of land exercises have been devised, and many of them have been used with apparent success over the years. However, weight training and exercises with pulley weights appear to be the most valuable of the land exercise methods. The value of weight training lies in the opportunity it affords to work against greater resistance than water offers, and, even more important, the amount of resistance can be precisely measured. A progressive resistance program can be worked out with great accuracy. Swimmers and coaches have long placed a high value on exercises with the pulley weights. Because the pulleys provide flexibility of movement, stroke action can be simulated, thus placing emphasis on the muscle groups·that most contribute to propulsion.

As you embark on your land exercise program, it's important to remember that you are exercising to become a better swimmer. It's essential to keep your weight-training program geared to your swimming ambitions. Above all, avoid building up great bulk that could cut down on your endurance.

Early season. For the most part, land exercises are emphasized during the very early part of the season. Later on the exercises are usually eliminated, although more and more swimmers maintain at least a reduced land exercise program throughout the season. They feel that such exercises are needed to maintain a level of strength that swimming alone cannot provide.

The early season is also the time for intensive attention to technique. Needed and even radical corrections are made in the start, turn, and stroke mechanics. Changes in technique, necessary as they are to future performance, almost always bring about a temporary setback, but in the interest of future performance you can easily afford a temporary setback during the early season. Even as the season progresses you will continue to keep an eye on technique, but changes will be relatively minor. Any big changes are made during the early season.

The body can make remarkable adjustments to the tasks confronting it. That is, of course, the secret of modern training methods. But the body has to be given a chance. You have to build gradually and progressively. A workout day that would be highly valuable in midseason could be harmful in early season. The body simply would not be ready for it. In brief, you don't go all out in your first workouts, but increase the workload gradually as the body gets used to it and is ready for more.

Coaches use the terms "quantity" and "quality." "Quantity" means a lot of mileage carried out at a relatively slow pace. "Quality" means high-speed work, often at racing speed or better. During the season there is a gradual movement from quantity to quality. The early season emphasizes slower work but plenty of it. Stamina is built, and in this way the body becomes prepared for the faster work to come.

Components of a workout. We know that the preparation for top swimming requires a lot of swimming. We also know that the workload has to be progressive—with increasing amounts of work as the body is ready for it. But even further, we've learned a great deal about how the work is best applied.

The ingredients used to formulate a workout are discussed in the other swim books in this series.* Do try to look at these books. An understanding of how a training program is put together heightens your enthusiasm and

---

* See *Freestyle Swimming, Breaststroke Swimming,* and *Backstroke Swimming,* from the Viking Library of Sports Skills.

tends to make you and your coach partners in a success plan. The basic ingredients of a workout are: interval training, repetition training, overdistance, fartlek, pulling, and kicking.

Both interval training and repetition training come from the world of running. The methods were worked out on a scientific basis and then put into practice, with startling results. World records were shattered. The methods had to be adopted by all ambitious runners, and swimmers quickly followed. There is still some natural confusion about the difference between the two methods, because there are similarities. Both make use of parts of the race. For example, if you are training for the 440-yard race, segments of 100 yards could be selected, and you would then carry out a series of repetitions of 100 yards with rest intervals between repetitions. It is the length of the rest interval that most distinguishes the two methods. The original research and theory behind interval training were based on pulse rate, and the rest interval is meant to provide only a partial recovery. For example, at the end of a repeat your pulse might be 180, and the rest interval might permit the pulse rate to drop down to 120, still well above that of the normal resting state. Although the amount of drop in pulse rate is the theoretical basis for determining the duration of the rest interval, an actual practice dependence is on the clock, experience suggesting about the right amount of time for the heart rate to drop to the desired level.

Repetition training allows for fuller rest intervals between repeats. There is almost complete recovery. Hence, the repetitions can be swum faster, at racing speed or usually faster. There is great flexibility in setting the distance and number of repetitions to be swum.

Overdistance is just what the name implies. You swim farther—sometimes a lot farther—than your racing distance. In running, a miler finds it valuable to run marathons at different points in his training. Overdistance is for stamina. There is no contribution to strength. Other methods, such as interval training and repetition training, also build stamina and appear to do so more quickly than overdistance, yet there is evidence that the stamina created by overdistance stays with you longer.

Fartlek originated in Sweden and means "speed play." Substantial distances are covered at widely varying rates of speed. In running, the speed will vary all the way from walking and jogging to sprinting. At any one moment speed pretty much depends on impulse—the way you feel—so in a sense fartlek is an escape from the rigidly set training routine. Even though fartlek doesn't lend itself to swimming as it does to running, it has a significant place in the swimmer's training schedule, adding variety while contributing to endurance.

Pulling and kicking are standard components of the workout program. As mentioned earlier, they are essentially strength-building methods. If the legs are tied, the arms have to do all the work of propulsion. The resistance encountered by the arms is greater than in normal swimming, and the activity thus becomes strength-building. The same holds true for the legs when a kickboard is used. The arms make no contribution, and the legs get the overload. Pulling and kicking have an additional value in that with the arms or legs isolated greater concentration can be given to technique.

Although pulling and kicking are components of a workout, they can be combined with other components. For example, both can be carried out within a framework of interval training or repetition training.

Putting the components together. Just as a finite number of musical notes can produce an infinity of melodies, so the components of a workout can produce an endless variety of daily schedules. The great coach is part scientist and part artist. He is familiar with the components, and in putting them together to form your workouts, he takes into account a number of factors, such as the time available, the season, your event, your age and conditioning. Also, the coach is concerned with mental factors. From the strictly physical point of view, similar workouts day in and day out could do the job, but monotony and boredom are damaging. Workouts are therefore varied to sustain interest and enthusiasm.

The clock. Modern training methods depend heavily on using a clock. In most pools a large clock with a stopwatch face is placed so that it can easily be read from the water. You quickly get used to working with the clock and are able to carry out a full workout assignment on your own. Although the clock is intended primarily for workouts that contribute to endurance, there is an important by-product. Constant working with the clock makes you increasingly sensitive to pace—and, of course, a sense of pace is a needed asset in competition. The use of the big clock yields still another happy result. Your coach, because he is not pinned down by his stopwatch, is freer to make observations and to give individual help where needed.

The main portion of your workouts will almost always require use of the clock. There will be some sessions when you are on your own, but most of the time your coach will have your workout all ready for you. It will probably be posted. To save space and time he will use some system of shorthand or abbreviations. It won't take long to get used to his methods of communication. The instructions concerning the clock will depend upon whether interval training or repetition training is being used. When interval training is being used, the time between repeats will be specified. For example, if your task is to carry out a series of 50-yard repeats, you may be asked to start one on every minute. The actual swimming and the rest period combine for a total of one minute. In repetition training both the time of the repeat and the time of the rest period are timed separately.

Grouping. In drawing up workout plans for the team, the coach may group the swimmers in various ways and then from time to time shift the groupings. Groupings can be made on the basis of age, experience, stroke, and distance to be swum. And, of course, there can be days when everyone gets about the same general workout. It's helpful and stimulating to work with a group carrying out the same assignments. But it isn't entirely necessary. As long as you have the clock and a lane or even half a lane to swim in, you carry out an individual workout.

Much of your early-season work can be carried out with the freestylers. Modern conditioning for swimming depends heavily on piling up mileage. Because the butterfly is a strenuous stroke, it doesn't lend itself well to the great distances needed in early practice sessions. Hence, freestyle is used for the bulk of the endurance work. As the season moves on, the coach will very likely change the groupings, and you will be working more and more with swimmers in your own event. There will be increased attention to your specialty stroke. Also the work will be faster.

Achievement. It is surely clear that the common denominator in great athletic achievement is work—and, of course, intelligently guided work. Many would like it otherwise, but it just doesn't happen that way. The most talented swimmer in the world, if he doesn't work, will be badly beaten by the average swimmer who does work. The term "work" has come to have many meanings for different people. It touches off all sorts of emotional reactions. Of course, the great achievers are the ones who are enthusiastic. To them work is enjoyable. But even so, in every effort toward great achievement there will be days when the going seems tough —boring and even painful. That's the reality of achievement. Every great swimmer knows this and accepts it as part of the price. He also knows that the price is well worth paying.